This book belongs to

_____

The China Doll

D.M. Rosner

Illustrations by Robert Jones

Jigsaw Press
Sun River, Montana

The China Doll

Text copyright © 2007 by D.M. Rosner

Illustrations copyright © 2007 by Robert Jones

No part of this book may be reproduced in any manner, stored in any retrieval system, or transmitted by any means—including, but not limited to, electronic, mechanical, photocopying, audio or video—without express written consent of the copyright owners, except in the case of brief quotationss embodied in critical articles or reviews.

For information address: Editor, Jigsaw Press, P.O. Box 136, Sun River, Montana, 59483

ISBN: 978-1-934340-99-8

Library of Congress Control Number: 2007924306

Publisher's Cataloguing in Publication Data
Rosner, Dawn M.
    The china doll / D. M. Rosner; illustrated by Robert Jones.
    p. cm.
    ISBN 9781934340998
    Summary: A new doll helps Emily learn that differences may hide wonderful surprises.
    Designed to teach children about their peers with autism; includes parents'/educators' section.
[1. Autism--Fiction. 2. Friendship--Fiction. 3. Dolls--Fiction.] I. Jones, Robert S. II. Title.

PZ7.R71952 Ch 2007

[E]--dc22   2007924306

Proudly manufactured in the United States of America

Jigsaw Press

Sun River, Montana

www.jigsawpress.com

*For Nicky and Kyle;
and everyone who loves somebody
with autism.*

Emily had the most amazing doll collection you have ever seen, dolls of all shapes, sizes, and colors— one hundred forty nine of them all together.

One day, her mother gave her a new one, a sweet little boy doll in a silk shirt and pants.

Emily reached for him, excited, but her mother said, "This doll is special. He's not what you might expect."

2

At first, Emily was a little nervous about playing with the new doll. She sat and looked at him awhile.

He had a hand-sewn, stuffed body, and his arms, legs, and face were delicate china. His painted blue eyes had a happy sparkle in them, even if they didn't quite look back at hers, but as far as she could tell, there was nothing all that different about him.

She brought some of her other dolls down from their shelf to play with him.

"You stand here," she told the china doll, propping him up against her dresser—but unlike her other dolls, this one didn't listen to her. He dropped down and sat however he chose, as if she wasn't playing with him at all.

Emily didn't like that very much, and so she left him sitting there while she played with the other dolls.

The china doll seemed happy enough sitting on his own, but after a while Emily felt a little sorry for him, and decided to try again.

"What you need is a trip to the ice cream stand," she said with a nod.

She took him in one hand, a curly-haired girl doll in the other, and walked them side-by-side across the green oval rug of her pretend park.

But with each of his little steps, the doll's arms flapped up and down, and his china legs made a strange noise when they clinked together.

Emily stopped and frowned at him. None of her other dolls did that.

"Maybe you'll do better with another boy," said Emily.

So she tried to make him play chase with a soldier doll, but that didn't work, either. The soldier's hand caught on the doll's fragile threads, and the stitching came undone.

"Oh, you're no good at all!" she hollered. Snatching him up, she stomped from the room and brought the doll to her mother.

"I don't like this one," said Emily. "I can't play with him like my other dolls, and he falls apart too easily."

Her mother took the doll and gently mended the torn seams. "Just because he's different, that doesn't mean you can't enjoy him. Look closely at his face—do you see the happy smile? And look…"

She pulled open the silk shirt. Beneath it shone a real ruby heart set into the soft fabric body.

Emily's eyes widened in surprise. "I didn't notice that."

Her mother smiled. "Of course not—you didn't look. I'll bet there's a lot you don't know about him yet. Why don't you give him another chance?"

Emily carried him back to her room.

"I guess we can find a way to play together," she told him. She put on some music, and found that he made a fun dance partner.

While they whirled their way around the room, she noticed that the happy little sparkle in his eyes came from real diamonds, and wondered what other surprises she would find in time.

A Note For Children:

Like china dolls, boys and girls with autism seem at first like any other kids you meet, but they don't act the same. Sometimes they won't answer you when you talk to them, or might repeat what you say. Sometimes they do things that seem mean or rude. Often, they get upset when something doesn't happen the way they think it should, or if you touch a toy they like, or if there's too much noise or confusion around them.

Just like Emily's china doll, boys and girls with autism are full of surprises, and even though they may have trouble talking, or might do things you don't understand, you can still have fun together. Give them a chance—you might be surprised at what you find when you do!

For Parents and Educators:

What is Autism?

Autism is a neurological disability affecting approximately 1 in 150 children born in the United States today.

Common symptoms include delayed speech, repetitive gestures, poor social skills, and trouble coping with change or frustration. Unusual behaviors and tantrums are often the only visible signs of autism.

Autism is not limited to extreme disability, either. Both Albert Einstein and Sir Isaac Newton exhibited signs of autism.

Facilitating Interaction and Understanding

There is no single set of symptoms that defines autism for every child; each one is a little different, and it will take some time to find the best way to interact with him or her.

Here are some ideas to make it easier for other children to understand and interact with their peers with autism:

• Explain that the hardest thing for most children with autism is understanding other people. They sometimes do things that are misunderstood (like stomping on a sand castle or knocking down a block building). They aren't being mean—they simply don't realize their actions will upset others.

• Remind them that everyone is better at some things than others, and even though talking and interacting are difficult for the child with autism, he or she may do other things very well.

- Be sure the children have gotten the attention of the child with autism before trying to interact with him or her. Explain that although the child sometimes seems as though he or she is deaf or ignoring people, it may be because he or she doesn't realize you are trying to interact. Often, it helps to stand right in front of the child, use his or her name, and say, "Look at me," before speaking. Even so, some children with autism will not respond to any verbal commands; if that is the case, be sure the other children know this, so they don't get angry when they don't receive a response.

- Have them ask permission from the child before trying to play with any toys the child was using, or before trying to touch him or her.

- Explain that some children with autism are oversensitive to touch, loud noises, or bright lights. If the child has sensory issues like these, he or she may either withdraw from the source (covering the ears or hiding), or may get upset by it. Not all children with autism share the same sensitivities, and some have no noticeable sensory issues at all, so be sure to take your cues from the child with whom you are working.

- Try to find activities in which the child with autism can easily participate. Music, puzzles, ball-playing, drawing, and non-contact chase games are a few ideas.
- Keep activities short and varied. Many children with autism have short attention spans, and variety will help hold their attention.

To learn more about autism, visit www.autismgear.com and click on "Links" for an up-to-date list of resources.

About the Author

D.M. Rosner is the mother of two beautiful boys, one of whom has autism. Bothered by the lack of general public understanding about autism, she started building awareness by designing t-shirts and handout cards to educate the adults she encountered, but also wanted to find a way to reach out to the children who misunderstand those with autism. *The China Doll*, her first children's book, is the result. Her other published work includes essays, articles, and short stories.

For more information about Ms. Rosner, please visit www.dmrosner.com.

For t-shirts, handout cards, and other autism awareness items designed by Ms. Rosner, please visit www.autismgear.com.

About the Illustrator

Robert Jones was born, raised, and educated in New York State. An early career in package design led to advertising and, ultimately, illustrating.

His work in the past includes GAMES magazine, toy packages for American Greetings (*Those Characters From Cleveland*), and nearly 30 school lunch kits for Aladdin Industries and Thermos Corporation (*Dukes of Hazzard*, *Grizzly Adams*, and *Magic Kingdom* to name a few).

Recently, Bob has freelanced for many Nashville publishing houses, producing children's illustrations for the United Methodist Publishing House, LifeWay, Abbey Press, and Thomas Nelson Publications.

Bob makes his home in Hermitage, Tennessee with his wife, Severina, and Bess the Beagle, on property once grazed by Andrew Jackson's cows. Three boys and their families live in close proximity, while his daughter practices law with the Smithsonian.

Please visit Bob on the Web at: www.PrintsRobert.com

D.M. Rosner would like to thank
her sons Nicky and Kyle, and the rest of her family;
M.L. Bushman; Sean Capelle; Nancy Vaine; Linda Meikle;
Betsy Cahours; and all of The 6' Ferret Writers' Group
members throughout the years;
and last, but not least, Bob Jones for his generous spirit and
truly amazing artwork.

A ***very special thank you*** goes out to teachers, speech
therapists, occupational therapists, and everyone else
who willingly gives their time to work with special needs
children around the world.

For the missing pieces of your reading puzzle...

Jigsaw Press
www.jigsawpress.com